GIRL, PRAY

A Real Girl's Guide to Talking to God

Cynthia M. Pillow

Girl, Pray © January 2026

By Cynthia M. Pillow

Published in the United States of America by

ChosenButterflyPublishing LLC

www.ChosenButterflyPublishing.com

ISBN: 978-1-945377-58-7

First Edition Printing

Printed in the United States of America

January 2026

Dedications

To every girl who has ever felt unheard, overlooked, or unsure of how to pray—this is for you.

May you discover the power in your voice, the peace in God's presence, and the purpose in your prayers.

And to my daughter Celena — your light, your strength, and your heart have inspired every page.

Table of Contents

Foreword

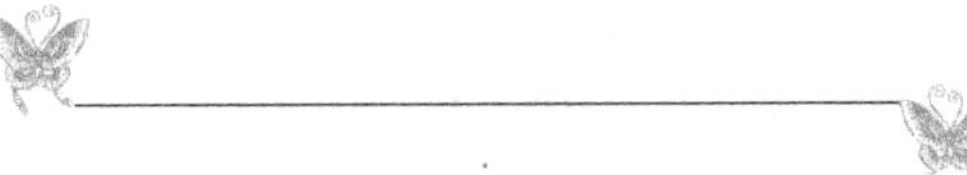

Pastor Kimberely R. Allen

There are moments when God gives someone a message that meets a generation right where they are, and *Girl, Pray* is one of those moments. Cynthia Pillow has written a treasure for every young girl who's ever wondered if her prayers matter. In a world full of noise, pressure, and comparison, *Girl, Pray* becomes a quiet place where teenage hearts can breathe, believe, and talk to God in a way that feels real.

On the very first page, Cynthia's voice is genuine and filled with grace. She doesn't talk at girls; she talks to them, and that makes all the difference. Her words feel like a big sister's encouragement mixed with a mother's wisdom and a friend's understanding. She shows girls that prayer isn't about perfect words or fancy phrases, it's about honest conversation with a God who loves them just as they are. Each devotion, reflection, and journaling prompt guides the reader through real issues that teen girls face: anxiety, friendship, struggles, self-worth, and learning how to trust God's timing. What I love most is how *Girl, Pray* reminds every reader that God cares about their whole story, even the parts that feel messy or misunderstood.

This isn't just a devotional; it's an experience. It is a mirror that reflects identity, a friend that listens without judgment, and a gentle lifeline that reminds girls they are never alone. Cynthia's transparent heart makes every page feel like an open door into prayer: simple, sincere, and powerful. So, to every young girl who opened this book: Know this. You are seen, loved, and heard. Your voice matters. Your prayers matter. And no matter what you face, you have a God who is listening.

Cynthia, thank you for being brave enough to write what girls need to hear and strong enough to say it with truth and tenderness. This book is more than words; it's a movement of prayer for a new generation.

With love and gratitude,

Pastor Kimberely R. Allen

Author: *Living in Two Worlds, Destined for Change, The Little Girl Within*

Preface

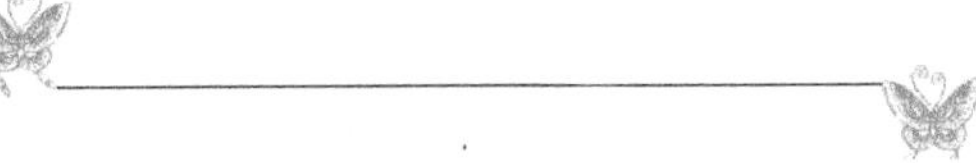

Hey Girl... Let's Talk

I don't know where you are right now, but I'm guessing it might look a little something like this:

You've got a lot on your mind. Maybe school's been crazy. Maybe your friendships are changing. Maybe there are things going on in your heart that you haven't told anyone about. Or maybe ... you're just tired of pretending you're okay when you're really not.

I see you, girl. And more importantly, God sees you. Not the version of you that shows up with a fake smile. Not the you that tries to have it all together. The real you. The unsure, messy, quiet, beautiful you. And guess what. He still wants to talk to you. Every day. About everything.

Let me tell you where my prayer journey started.

When I was a little girl, I used to watch my nana, my great-grandmother. After she finished dinner, she would quietly go upstairs to her room. I was always fascinated by that. I'd follow behind her and sit at the top of the steps, just outside her closed door. I could hear her talking, but there was no one else in the room.

One day, I got curious enough to ask her who she was talking to. She smiled and said, "I'm talking to God."

That moment stuck with me.

Eventually, she invited me into her room to pray with her. I knelt down beside her, listened to her heart pour out to God, and felt something I didn't have words for yet—peace. Power. Presence. And love.

That's where my love for prayer began.

And that's why I wrote **Girl, Pray**. Because I know what prayer can do. Because I know how much girls like you need it. And because I haven't seen many books that talk about prayer in a way that feels real and reachable.

This isn't a book of perfect prayers.

It's a book for real girls with real questions and real struggles.

So take a deep breath. Get your favorite pen. Open your heart.

You're about to discover that prayer isn't pressure, it's power. Let's talk, girl. Let's pray!

How to Use This Book

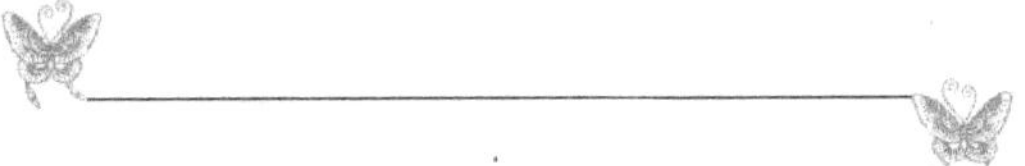

This book is your space—a mix of real talk, truth, and time with God. Each chapter includes a short devotional, a few reflection questions, a prayer, and a journaling prompt. Take your time. Go at your own pace. Some girls read a chapter a week. Others read one every day. You choose.

Here's a simple way to get the most out of this book:

1. Read the Scripture and devotional—highlight or underline what speaks to you.

2. Answer the reflection questions honestly—this is your heart space.

3. Pray the guided prayer out loud or in your head.

4. Use the journaling section to write, draw, pray, or just think.

You don't have to be perfect. You just have to be real. God is listening—and He's ready to meet you right where you are.

This Is How Prayer Works

The Lord's Prayer *Matthew 6:9–13 (NIV)*

The Lord's Prayer isn't just something we memorize—it's a powerful guide that shows us how to talk to God. Jesus gave us this model to help us understand the heart of prayer. Let's break it down, one line at a time:

1. **"Our Father in heaven, hallowed be your name"**

   Start your prayers by remembering who God is. He's your Father—and He's holy. Worship comes first.

2. **"Your kingdom come, your will be done, on earth as it is in heaven"**

   Invite God's will into your life. Trust His plans, even when they're different from yours.

3. **"Give us today our daily bread"**

   Ask God for what you need today. Not just stuff—but peace, strength, focus, or help.

4. **"Forgive us our debts, as we also have forgiven our debtors"**

    Ask for forgiveness and choose to forgive others too. Forgiveness frees your heart.

5. **"And lead us not into temptation, but deliver us from the evil one"**

    Ask God for guidance, strength, and protection. You're not in this alone.

6. **"For Yours is the Kingdom, and the Power, and the Glory Forever. Amen."**

    End your prayer with worship and thanksgiving, reminding you that God reigns over everything.

    Prayer isn't complicated. It's connection. Use this prayer as a pattern to grow more confident in talking to God every day.

Chapter 1

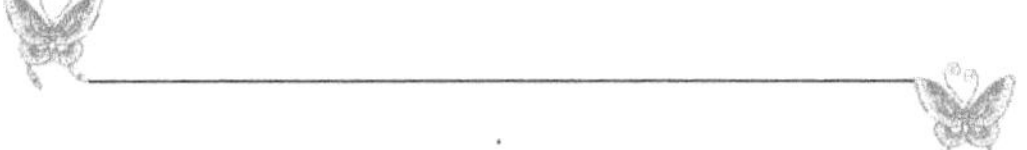

Girl, Just Talk to God—Words or Not

"In the same way, the Spirit helps us in our weakness. We do not know what we ought to pray for, but the Spirit Himself intercedes for us through wordless groans."
Romans 8:26 (NIV)

Just Be Real!

Have you ever wanted to pray but didn't know what to say? Maybe your prayers didn't sound "spiritual" enough or maybe the pain inside was too deep to put into words. Here's the truth, girl: prayer isn't about performance, it's about presence.

God doesn't need fancy words; He just wants your words. And even when you have no words at all, when all you have is silence, tears, or a sigh, He still understands. The Holy Spirit helps you pray when you can't find the language.

Let's Go Deeper

1. What keeps you from talking to God more often?

____

____

____

____

2. Have you ever tried to 'sound spiritual' when you prayed? Why?

____

____

____

____

3. How does it make you feel to know that God understands even in your silence?

____

____

____

____

Let's Pray

God, sometimes I don't know what to say. Sometimes I feel unsure or not good enough. Thank you that You're not asking for perfect words, You just want me. Teach me how to be real with You, whether through words, silence, or tears. Thank You for loving me just as I am. Amen.

Girl, Write This Down

Take a moment to write your honest thoughts to God. There's no right or wrong way to do this—just start where you are.

- What would you say to God right now if you could say anything without holding back?
- When words fail, how do you show your feelings, through journaling, tears, or silence?
- Write out a prayer, a letter, or even just bullet points of what's on your heart.

My Honest Thoughts

____

____

____

____

____

What I Am Praying For

____

____

____

____

What God Has Shown Me

Chapter 2

Is God Even Listening?

"This is the confidence we have in approaching God: that if we ask anything according to his will, he hears us. And if we know that he hears us—whatever we ask—we know that we have what we asked of him."
John 5:14–15 (NIV)

Silence Doesn't Mean Ignored

Let's be honest, waiting is hard, especially when you've been praying your heart out and feel like you're getting nothing but silence. You might even wonder, *Does God even care?* or, *Am I doing something wrong?* Girl, I've been there. But here's the truth you need to hold on to: God always hears you—even when you don't feel Him.

Sometimes God answers right away. Sometimes He says, "Wait." And other times, He's answering in ways you can't see yet. But He is never ignoring you. His silence is never absence. His delay is not a denial. God is working in the unseen, even when you feel unheard.

So don't stop praying just because you don't hear an echo. Keep showing up. Keep pouring out your heart. Because He's not ignoring you—He's inviting you to trust Him.

Real Talk

1. Have you ever felt like your prayers were ignored? What did you do?

____

____

____

____

____

2. What are you waiting on God for right now?

____

____

____

____

____

3. How can you choose faith even when the answer
    hasn't come?

____

____

____

____

____

Let's Pray

God, sometimes I feel like You're silent and that silence makes me wonder if You're really listening. But Your Word says You hear me. So even when I feel nothing, I choose to believe that You are near. Strengthen my heart while I wait. Help me trust that You are working behind the scenes for my good. Amen.

Girl, Write This Down

Write a prayer about something you've been waiting on or something you've been unsure about.

Let this be a space to be honest—even if that means saying, "God, I'm frustrated."

- God, I've been waiting for...
- It's hard to trust you right now because...
- Even when I don't see it, I choose to believe...

My Honest Thoughts

____

____

____

____

What I Am Praying For

____

____

____

____

What God Has Shown Me

____

____

____

____

Chapter 3

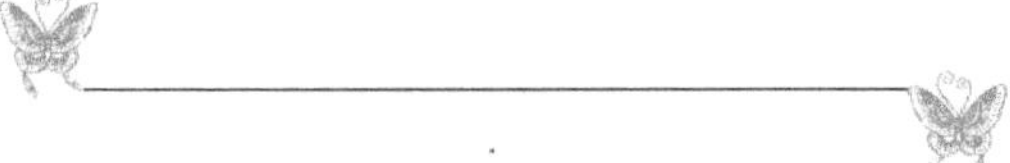

Girl, Listen Up, Prayer Is a Conversation

"My sheep listen to my voice; I know them, and they follow me." John 10:27 (NIV)

Prayer Is a Two-Way Conversation

Most of us think prayer is all about talking—but did you know it's also about listening? Prayer isn't just a monologue; it's a real conversation with the God who wants to speak into your life.

God speaks in different ways—through His Word, through people, through moments, and through that quiet nudge in your spirit. The question isn't if He's speaking; it's whether we're tuned in to hear Him.

You don't have to be a Bible scholar to hear God. You just need a quiet moment, an open heart, and a willingness to listen.

Heart Check

1. What do you think it means to hear God's voice?

____

____

____

____

____

2. When have you felt like God was speaking to you?

____

____

____

____

____

3. What could you do to quiet your world enough
    to listen?

____

____

____

____

____

Let's Pray

God, I talk to You a lot, but today I want to be quiet and listen. Help me to hear You—through Your Word, through peace, through whispers. I want to know Your voice. Speak to me in a way I'll understand. Amen.

Girl, Write This Down

Sit in stillness for a few minutes. Then write what comes to your heart. Don't overthink it, just be open.

- What do I feel like God is saying to me today?
- What Scripture or word keeps coming to mind?
- Write a prayer response to what you hear.

My Honest Thoughts

____

____

____

____

What I Am Praying For

____

____

____

____

What God Has Shown Me

____

____

____

____

Chapter 4

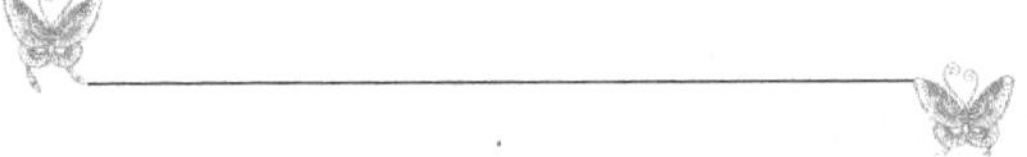

Prayers for the Mess, Drama, Mistakes, and All

"If we confess our sins, He is faithful and just and will forgive us our sins and purify us from all unrighteousness." 1 John 1:9 (NIV)

Bring the Mess to God

Life can be overwhelming—friend drama, school stress, family tension. On top of that, we sometimes create our own mess by making mistakes and choices we regret. Both can make us feel like prayer is the last thing we want to do.

But here's the truth: God isn't scared of your drama and He isn't shocked by your mistakes. He doesn't roll His eyes when you bring Him your chaos and He doesn't turn away when you confess your guilt. His love is bigger than your mess and His grace is stronger than your failures.

You don't have to wait until everything is fixed to talk to Him. Pray in the middle of the drama. Pray when you've messed up. Pray when you feel unworthy. That's when His peace and forgiveness meet you.

Let's Go Deeper

1. What kind of drama or stress has been weighing on your heart?

____

____

____

____

____

____

2. What's something you've felt too guilty or ashamed about to bring to God?

____

____

____

____

____

3. How can you invite God into both the chaos around you and the mistakes inside you?

____

____

____

____

____

____

Let's Pray

God, my life feels messy sometimes, whether from drama around me or mistakes I've made. But I know I can always come to You. Forgive me when I fall short and give me peace when I feel overwhelmed. Thank You for loving me, even when I feel unlovable. Amen.

Girl, Write This Down

Write about a situation that's been stressing you out or causing drama.

- God, here's what I need help with...

- I'm carrying guilt about...

- Help me let go of the stress and receive Your peace

My Honest Thoughts

____

____

____

____

What I Am Praying For

____

____

____

____

What God Has Shown Me

____

____

____

____

Chapter 5

When Fear Comes First

"So do not fear, for I am with you; do not be dismayed, for I am your God. I will strengthen you and help you; I will uphold you with my righteous right hand." Isaiah 41:10 (NIV)

Faith Doesn't Mean Fear Disappears

Fear is real—and it doesn't make you weak. It makes you human. God never said you wouldn't feel fear. He said you don't have to be *ruled* by it.

When fear shows up, you can pray through it. You can talk to the God who promises to be right there in the middle of the panic, the pressure, and the unknown.

You don't have to fake bravery with God. He knows your heart. And He promises to hold you through it all.

Real Talk

1. What's something that's been making you
   anxious or afraid?

____

____

____

____

____

2. How do you normally respond to fear?

____

____

____

____

____

3. What would it look like to pray through your fear
   instead of avoiding it?

____

____

____

____

____

Let's Pray

God, fear keeps showing up in my life. But I don't want to let it win. Remind me that You're with me and for me, even when I feel afraid. Replace my panic with peace and help me trust You more each day. Amen.

Girl, Write This Down

Write a prayer asking God to meet you in your fear.

- God, here's what I'm afraid of...
- I need Your courage for...
- I choose to trust You even though...

My Honest Thoughts

____

____

____

____

What I Am Praying For

____

____

____

____

What God Has Shown Me

____

____

____

____

Chapter 6

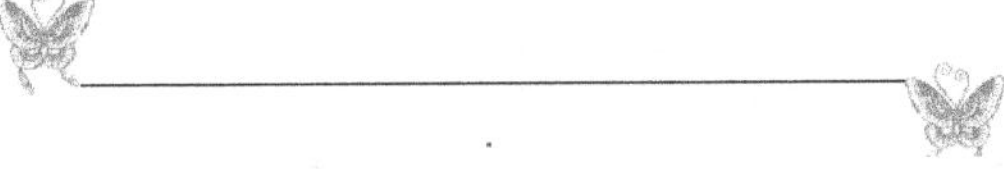

When God Says No

*"And we know that in all things God works
for the good of those who love him, who
have been called according to his purpose."*
Romans 8:28 (NIV)

The "No" That's Still Good

We all love a good "yes"—answered prayers, open doors, big blessings. But what happens when the answer is "no" or when it's not what we expected or hoped for?

Sometimes God's "no" is actually His protection. Sometimes it's His redirection. And sometimes it's just part of a bigger picture we can't see yet.

Trusting God when He says no takes faith. It means believing that His plan is still good, even when it doesn't feel good in the moment.

Real Talk

1. Have you ever felt disappointed by God's answer?

    ____

    ____

    ____

    ____

    ____

2. Can you think of a time when a "no" ended up being a blessing?

    ____

    ____

    ____

    ____

    ____

3. How can you trust God even when you don't understand?

    ____

    ____

    ____

    ____

    ____

Let's Pray

God, it's hard to hear "no" when I really want something. But I trust that You know what's best for me. Even when I don't understand, help me believe that You're still good and You're still working all things out for my good. Amen.

Girl, Write This Down

Write about a time when God's answer wasn't what you wanted.

- God, I didn't understand when...
- Looking back, I can see You were...
- Help me to trust You more when the answer is "no"

My Honest Thoughts

____

____

____

____

What I Am Praying For

____

____

____

____

What God Has Shown Me

____

____

____

Chapter 7

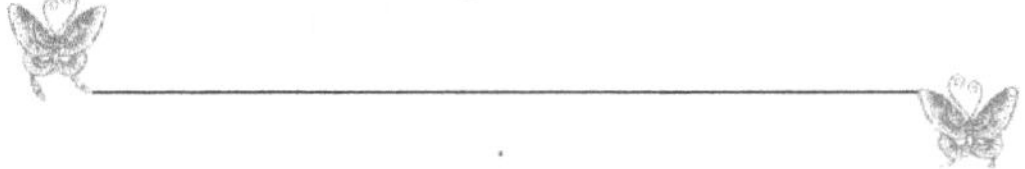

Pray for Her, Too

*"But I tell you, love your enemies and pray for
those who persecute you."*
Matthew 5:44 (NIV)

Love Through Prayer

It's easy to pray for our friends, but what about the
girl who talks about you behind your back? What
about the one who hurt you or left you out?

Jesus challenges us to pray even for those people—
not to excuse what they've done but to free
ourselves from the weight of bitterness.

When you pray for someone who hurt you, you invite
God into the healing. You open the door for peace—
not just with them but inside your own heart.

Heart Check

1. Who is someone who's been hard for you to love
    or forgive?

____

____

____

____

____

2. What would it look like to pray for them honestly?

____

____

____

____

____

3. How does praying for others change your
    own heart?

____

____

____

____

Let's Pray

God, I don't always want to pray for the people who've hurt me—but I know You've called me to love like You love. Help me to release the anger and instead lift them up to You. Do a work in their hearts and in mine. Amen.

Girl, Write This Down

Write a prayer for someone you find hard to love right now.

- God, it's hard to pray for...
- Help me to forgive and let go of...
- I choose to show love even when...

My Honest Thoughts

____

____

____

____

What I Am Praying For

____

____

____

____

What God Has Shown Me

____

____

____

____

Chapter 8

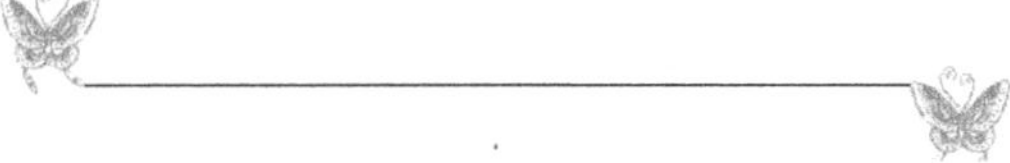

Worship Is Prayer, Too

*"Shout for joy to the Lord, all the earth.
Worship the Lord with gladness; come before
him with joyful songs." Psalm 100:1–2 (NIV)*

Let Your Worship Speak

Prayer doesn't always look like words. Sometimes, it looks like a song. A journal entry. A quiet moment of awe. Worship *is* a form of prayer.

When you sing, when you create, when you lift your heart to God—that's prayer too. It's your spirit connecting with His.

You don't need a stage or a microphone. You just need a heart that's open to praise. Let your worship rise. Let your life be a song.

Heart Check

1. What are some ways you naturally worship God?

____

____

____

____

2. How can you turn your everyday moments into worship?

____

____

____

____

3. What's one song that helps you feel close to God?

____

____

____

____

Let's Pray

God, thank You for the gift of worship. Help me to see that praise is prayer too. Let my life sing to You— in words, in silence, in art, in everything. Amen.

Girl, Write This Down

Create your own worship moment.

- Write a worship prayer or poem.
- List songs that help you feel God's presence.
- Describe how you feel when you're worshipping.

My Honest Thoughts

____

____

____

____

What I Am Praying For

____

____

____

____

What God Has Shown Me

____

____

____

____

Chapter 9

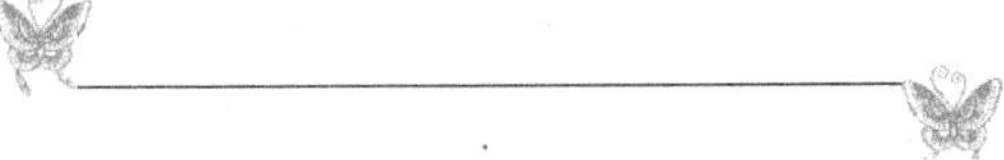

Girl, Stay Prayed Up

"Pray continually." 1 Thessalonians 5:17 (NIV)

Prayer Is a Lifestyle

Prayer isn't just a moment, it's a mindset. It's not just something you do at church or before bed. It's something you carry with you, all day, every day.

God wants to be part of your life, not just part of your emergencies. He wants to walk with you at school, at practice, during the hard times and the fun times.

Staying "prayed up" doesn't mean you're perfect, it just means you're consistent. Talk to Him throughout your day, like a friend who's always by your side.

Real Talk

1. When do you usually pray—and when do you forget?

____

____

____

____

____

2. What would it look like to include God in the little moments?

____

____

____

____

____

3. What might change if you stayed more connected to Him throughout your day?

____

____

____

____

Let's Pray

God, help me to stay close to You—not just when things are hard but always. Teach me to live in constant connection with You. Remind me that prayer is part of who I am, not just what I do. Amen.

Girl, Write This Down

Think about your daily routine and how you can include God in every part of it.

- God, be with me when I'm...
- Help me to remember You during...
- I want to build a lifestyle of prayer by...

My Honest Thoughts

____

____

____

____

What I Am Praying For

____

____

____

____

What God Has Shown Me

____

____

____

____

Chapter 10

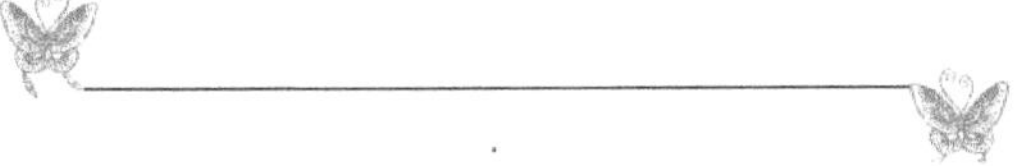

Praying with Purpose

"For I know the plans I have for you," declares the Lord, "plans to prosper you and not to harm you, plans to give you hope and a future." Jeremiah 29:11 (NIV)

You Were Born for This

You're not here by accident. God made you with purpose. He placed gifts, dreams, and fire inside of you that this world needs.

When you pray with purpose, you align your heart with heaven's plan. You begin to see yourself the way God sees you—not small or invisible but chosen and equipped.

Your prayers can change things. They can change *you*. So don't be afraid to pray big, bold prayers. You're talking to the One who created the stars.

Real Talk

1. What do you think God created you to do?

____

____

____

____

2. What gifts or dreams has He placed in your heart?

____

____

____

____

3. What would you pray for if you truly believed
    God could do anything?

____

____

____

____

Let's Pray

God, thank You for creating me with purpose. Show me the plans You have for my life. Give me courage to pray bold prayers and follow You fully. Use my life to make a difference. Amen.

Girl, Write This Down

Dream with God on paper today.

- God, I believe You created me to…
- One dream I have is…
- I trust You with my future because…

My Honest Thoughts

____

____

____

____

What I Am Praying For

____

____

____

____

What God Has Shown Me

____

____

____

____

Chapter 11

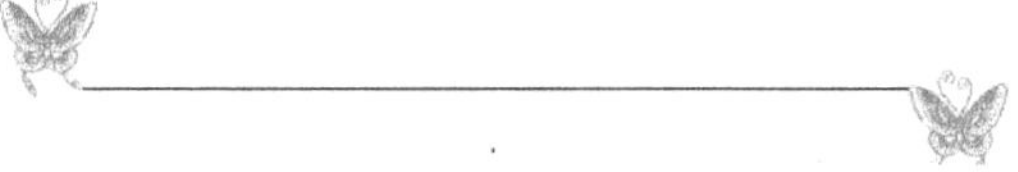

Faith in the Hallways

"Cast all your anxiety on him because he cares for you."1 Peter 1:7 (NIV)

Prayer Between Classes

Between homework, tests, group projects, and trying to keep up with everything else in life, school can feel like a pressure cooker. Sometimes it's not just the work — it's the people, the changes, or the feeling that you have to be "on" all the time.

The good news? God cares about all of it. He's not just the God of Sundays—He's the God of Mondays in math class and Wednesdays in the cafeteria. You can pray before a big test, when you're walking into a tough class, or even when you're sitting in the middle of one.

Prayer doesn't take the work away, but it does bring God into it. And with Him by your side, you're never walking those halls alone.

1. What's the hardest part of school for you right now?

____

____

____

____

____

2. How do you usually deal with school stress?

____

____

____

____

____

3. How can you make prayer part of your school day?

____

____

____

____

____

Let's Pray

God, You see the pressure I feel at school. You know when I'm stressed, tired, or overwhelmed. Help me to do my best and trust You with the rest. Be my peace in the chaos and my strength when I'm worn out. Amen.

Girl, Write This Down

- God, here's what's stressing me at school...
- Help me remember You when...
- One way I can pray during my school day is...

My Honest Thoughts

____

____

____

____

What I Am Praying For

____

____

____

____

What God Has Shown Me

____

____

____

____

Chapter 12

It's Not About the Likes

"Am I now trying to win the approval of human beings, or of God? ... If I were still trying to please people, I would not be a servant of Christ." — Galatians 1:10 (NIV)

Living Unfiltered

Scrolling can be fun—but it can also make you feel like you're not enough. Social media has a way of making everyone's life look perfect and comparison can sneak in fast. You might feel pressure to look a certain way, act a certain way, or post just the right thing to get attention.

God wants you to remember that your value isn't measured in likes, views, or followers. You were already chosen and loved before you ever posted a thing. When you feel the pull to perform, pause and pray. Ask God to help you see yourself through His eyes—not through a filter.

Heart Check

1. How does social media affect the way you feel about yourself?

____

____

____

____

____

2. Have you ever changed something about yourself online to fit in?

____

____

____

____

3. How can prayer help you stay true to who God made you to be?

____

____

____

____

Let's Pray

God, sometimes I care way too much about what people online think of me. Help me to remember that Your approval is what matters most. Protect my heart from comparison and teach me to use social media in a way that honors You. Amen.

Girl, Write This Down

- God, this is how I feel after scrolling...
- Help me to remember my worth comes from...
- One way I can use my social media for good is...

My Honest Thoughts

____

____

____

____

What I Am Praying For

____

____

____

____

What God Has Shown Me

____

____

____

____

Chapter 13

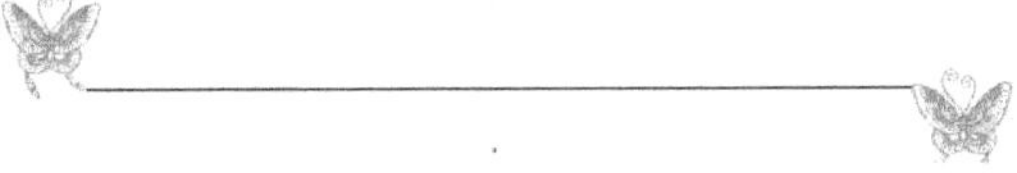

Mirror Talk (Image)

"I praise you because I am fearfully and wonderfully made; your works are wonderful; I know that full well." — Psalm 139:14 (NIV)

Seeing What God Sees

It's easy to focus on the parts of yourself you wish you could change—especially when you see endless pictures of "perfect" bodies online or hear comments from others. But God created you with intention, detail, and love. Every part of you has His fingerprints on it.

Your worth isn't found in your size, shape, or style—it's found in being His. When negative thoughts about your body show up, turn them into prayers. Thank Him for the body that lets you laugh, run, dance, and live. Ask Him to help you see yourself the way He does—beautiful, beloved, and enough.

Real Talk

1. What's something you've been insecure about?

____

____

____

____

____

2. How has comparing yourself to others affected you?

____

____

____

____

____

3. How can you thank God for your body today?

____

____

____

____

Let's Pray

God, thank You for making me exactly as You wanted me to be. Help me to see myself through Your eyes, not through the world's standards. Teach me to love the body You've given me and to use it to glorify You. Amen.

Girl, Write This Down

- God, here's what I've been feeling about my body...
- Thank You for creating me with...
- I choose to believe today that I am...

My Honest Thoughts

____

____

____

____

What I Am Praying For

____

____

____

____

What God Has Shown Me

____

____

____

____

Chapter 14

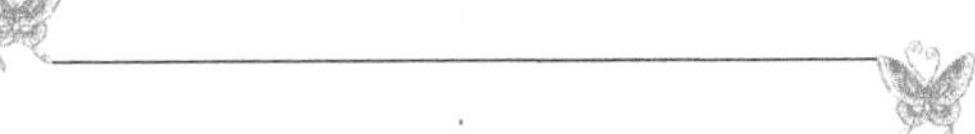

Stand Out, Don't Blend In

"Do not be misled: 'Bad company corrupts good character.'" — 1 Corinthians 15:33 (NIV)

Courage over Comfort

Friends can be amazing—but sometimes they can also lead you into choices you know aren't right. Peer pressure doesn't always shout; sometimes it whispers, "Everyone's doing it," or, "Don't be lame."

God calls you to stand strong, even when it's unpopular. That takes courage, but you're not doing it alone. When you feel pressured to do something that doesn't honor God, stop and pray. Ask Him for the strength to walk away, the wisdom to make the right choice, and the confidence to stand out instead of blending in.

Heart Check

1. When have you felt pressured to do something you didn't want to do?

____

____

____

____

2. What makes it hard to say no in those moments?

____

____

____

____

3. How can you prepare yourself to stand strong next time?

____

____

____

____

Let's Pray

God, sometimes it's hard to say no when everyone else is saying yes. Give me the courage to choose what's right and the strength to walk away from what's wrong. Help me to surround myself with friends who will encourage me in my faith. Amen.

Girl, Write This Down

- God, here's a situation where I feel pressured…
- Give me the courage to…
- I choose to follow You even when…

My Honest Thoughts

____

____

____

____

What I Am Praying For

____

____

____

What God Has Shown Me

____

____

____

____

Chapter 15

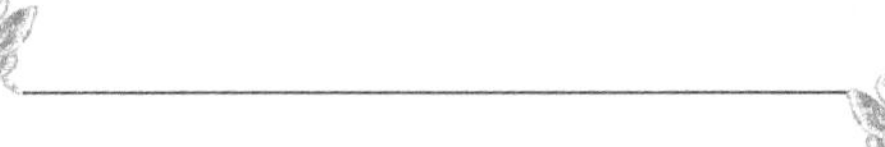

Bridges, Not
Walls (Relationships/Parents)

"Honor your father and your mother, so that you may live long in the land the Lord your God is giving you." — Exodus 20:12 (NIV)

Choosing Connection over Conflict

Let's be real—parent-and-teen relationships can get messy. You love each other, but sometimes it feels like you're speaking different languages. Rules, curfews, expectations, and opinions can clash.

But here's the thing—God designed family for connection, not constant conflict. Even when you don't agree, prayer can help you see each other through His eyes. It can soften misunderstandings and open the door for real conversations instead of just arguments.

You can pray for patience when tensions are high, for courage to speak honestly without disrespect, and for love to lead the way. Every prayer you pray is like building a bridge instead of stacking another brick in a wall between you.

Heart Check

1. What's one thing you wish your parents understood about you right now?

____

____

____

____

____

____

2. What's one thing you could try to understand better about them?

____

____

____

____

____

____

3. How can prayer help you have a healthier relationship?

____

____

____

____

____

____

Let's Pray

God, thank You for the family You've given me. Sometimes it's hard for us to see eye to eye, but I want our relationship to grow stronger. Help me to show respect and love, even when we disagree. Give us both patience and open hearts. Amen.

Girl, Write This Down

- God, here's where I feel misunderstood...

- Help me to show love by...

- I want to pray for my parent(s) today by asking You to...

My Honest Thoughts

____

____

____

____

What I Am Praying For

____

____

____

____

What God Has Shown Me

____

____

____

____

Chapter 16

Strong Inside and Out (Health/Physical)

"Do you not know that your bodies are temples of the Holy Spirit, who is in you, whom you have received from God? You are not your own; you were bought at a price. Therefore, honor God with your bodies." — 1 Corinthians 6:19–20 (NIV)

Caring for God's Temple

Taking care of your body isn't about trying to look a certain way—it's about honoring God with the gift He gave you. The choices you make with food, rest, and movement affect your energy, your focus, and even your mood.

But health isn't just physical. It's also about balance—making time to rest, handling stress, and guarding what you allow into your mind and heart. God wants you to live strong inside and out.

When you pray about your health, you're asking God to help you make wise choices, to give you strength when you feel weak, and to remind you that your worth is not in how you look but in Whose you are.

Heart Check

1. How do you usually feel about taking care of your body?

____

____

____

____

____

____

2. What's one healthy habit you want to grow in (food, exercise, sleep, or balance)?

____

____

____

____

____

____

3. How could prayer help you stay consistent with your health goals?

____

____

____

____

____

____

Let's Pray

God, thank You for the body You gave me. Help me to take care of it in a way that honors You—with the food I eat, the way I move, and the rest I take. Remind me that my health is not about perfection but about living in a way that glorifies You. Amen.

Girl, Write This Down

- • God, here's one area of my health I want to give to You...
- • Help me to make better choices when...
- • I want to honor You with my body by...

My Honest Thoughts

____

____

____

____

What I Am Praying For

____

____

____

____

What God Has Shown Me

____

____

____

____

Chapter 17

Real Talk About Relationships (Boys)

"Above all else, guard your heart, for everything you do flows from it."
— Proverbs 4:23 (NIV)

Healthy vs. Toxic

Relationships are a big part of life, whether it's friendships, crushes, or dating. God cares about who you connect your heart with. The right relationships can encourage your faith and bring joy. The wrong ones can leave you drained, hurt, or far from who God created you to be.

It's normal to want love and connection, but not every relationship is healthy. Toxic relationships, those full of pressure, manipulation, or disrespect, can harm your heart and your future. God doesn't want you stuck in something that makes you feel small, scared, or unloved.

He calls you to relationships that reflect His love: honest, safe, respectful, and life giving. Real love never asks you to compromise your worth.

Heart Check

1. What do you value most in a healthy relationship?

\
\
\
\
\
\

2. Have you ever noticed red flags in a friendship or dating relationship? What did you do?

\
\
\
\
\
\

3. How can you guard your heart while still opening yourself up to love and friendship?

____

____

____

____

____

____

____

Let's Pray

Lord, help me to guard my heart and honor You in my relationships. Help me to see clearly what is healthy and what's harmful. Help me to wait for the right time and the right person and never to forget my worth in You. Amen.

Girl, Write This Down

- Teach me how to guard my heart while still loving others
- God, this is what I want in my future relationships...
- Show me the red flags I need to watch for

My Honest Thoughts

____

____

____

____

What I Am Praying For

____

____

____

____

What God Has Shown Me

____

____

____

____

Chapter 18

Finding My Place (Relationships/Blended Family)

"How good and pleasant it is when God's people live together in unity!"
— Psalm 133:1 (NIV)

Blended Families and New Beginnings

Being part of a blended family can bring both blessings and challenges. Adjusting to stepparents, stepsiblings, or different households isn't always easy. But God reminds us that unity and love are possible even in complicated situations.

You don't have to have it all figured out right away. What matters most is showing respect, practicing patience, and leaning on God's love. He can help create peace in your heart and your home, even when things feel confusing.

Heart Check

1. What do you find most challenging about being in a blended family?

____

____

____

____

____

2. How can you show love and respect in your home?

____

____

____

____

____

3. What does unity look like to you in your family?

____

____

____

____

____

Let's Pray

Lord, thank You for my family, even with its challenges. Help me to show love and respect in my home. Give me patience and understanding and teach me to trust that You can bring unity in every situation. Amen.

Girl, Write This Down

- One positive thing about my family is...
- One way I can help bring unity to my home is...
- A prayer I have for my family is...

My Honest Thoughts

____

____

____

____

What I Am Praying For

____

____

____

____

What God Has Shown Me

____

____

____

____

Chapter 19

Just Me (the Only Child)

"God sets the lonely in families."
— Psalm 68:6 (NIV)

Being an Only Child

Being the only child in your family can feel both special and lonely at times. You might love the attention and space, but sometimes you may wish for a sibling to share life with. God reminds us that He places us in families for a reason and He never leaves us without love.

Even if you don't have siblings, God provides friendships and community to remind you that you are never truly alone. Your story matters and God has given you a unique role in your family.

Heart Check

1.   What do you like most about being an only child?

____

____

____

____

____

2. What challenges do you face without siblings?

____

____

____

____

____

3. How has God placed other people in your life to remind you that you're not alone?

____

____

____

____

____

Let's Pray

God, thank You for my family and for the people You've placed in my life. When I feel lonely, remind me that I am never truly alone. Help me to see the blessings of being an only child and the purpose You have for me. Amen.

Girl, Write This Down

- Something I love about my family is...
- When I feel lonely, I will remind myself that...
- God, thank You for placing these people in my life...

My Honest Thoughts

____

____

____

____

What I Am Praying For

____

____

____

____

____

What God Has Shown Me

____

____

____

____

Chapter 20

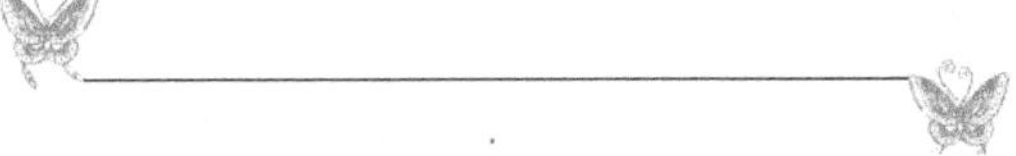

When the Mind Feels Heavy (Mental Health)

"Cast all your anxiety on him because he cares for you." — 1 Peter 5:7 (NIV)

Caring for Your Mental Health

Sometimes life feels overwhelming; school, friendships, family, and expectations can pile up until it feels like too much to carry. Mental health struggles like anxiety, depression, or just feeling weighed down are real and they don't make you weak or less spiritual. They make you human.

God cares about every part of you, including your mental health. He invites you to cast your cares on Him, not because He expects you to figure it all out alone but because He wants to walk with you through it. It's okay to ask for help—from a parent, a mentor, a counselor, or a trusted friend. You don't have to face the battle in silence.

Remember, even heroes in the Bible like Elijah and David experienced deep sadness and cried out to God in their lowest moments. God was faithful then and He is faithful now. Your mental health matters to Him.

Heart Check

1. What thoughts or feelings have been heavy on your mind lately?

____

____

____

____

____

2. Who can you talk to when you feel weighed down?

____

____

____

____

____

____

3. What does it mean to you to cast your cares on God?

____

____

____

____

____

____

____

Let's Pray

God, sometimes my mind feels heavy and my heart feels tired. Thank You for caring about me, even when I don't have the words to explain how I feel. Help me to trust You with my struggles and to remember that I'm not alone. Surround me with people who can listen and remind me of Your truth. Amen.

Girl, Write This Down

- God, here are the things that make my mind feel heavy...
- One healthy way I can take care of my mind and body this week is...
- The person I feel safe talking to about my feelings is...

My Honest Thoughts

____

____

____

____

What I Am Praying For

____

____

____

____

What God Has Shown Me

____

____

____

Chapter 21

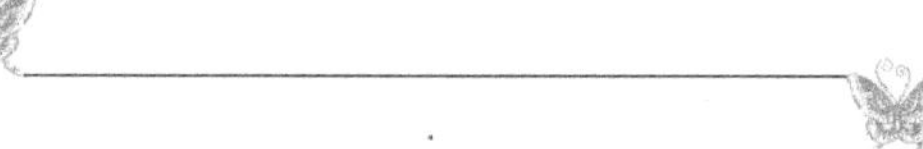

Lost Faith

When Believing Feels Impossible

What if you've stopped believing in God? Or maybe you were raised in church but deep down you don't know if you believe anymore. You see the hurt in the world, the struggles in your own life, and you wonder: *If God is real, where is He?*

Losing faith feels heavy, but it doesn't make you a lost cause. Many people in the Bible wrestled with disbelief—even Thomas, one of Jesus' own disciples, said he wouldn't believe unless he saw proof. And Jesus didn't reject him. Instead, He showed up.

God's love isn't canceled out by your doubt. Even if you feel done with Him, He is never done with you.

Faith isn't about never questioning; it's about being honest enough to admit where you are and being open to let God meet you there.

If you've lost faith, start here: be real with God. Say, "I don't even know if You're real, but if You are, show me who You are." He's not afraid of your questions. He's not offended by your doubts. He is patient, present, and waiting.

Heart Check

1. What makes it hardest for you to believe in God right now?

____

____

____

____

____

2. Are there moments in the past where you felt like He was real to you?

____

____

____

____

3. What would it take for you to feel open to faith again?

____

____

____

____

____

____

Let's Pray

God, I don't even know if I believe in You right now. I feel like I've lost my faith and I don't know how to get it back. If You're real, meet me in my doubts. Show me who You are in a way I can understand. And if I've walked away, thank You for never walking away from me. Amen.

Girl, Write This Down

- God, here's where my faith feels lost...
- If You're real, this is what I need You to show me...
- One small step I can take to open my heart again is...

My Honest Thoughts

What I Am Praying For

What God Has Shown Me

Chapter 22

When the Hurt Feels Too Heavy (Grief)

"Blessed are those who mourn, for they will be comforted." — Matthew 5:4 (NIV)

Holding On Through Loss

Losing someone you love, whether through death, broken relationships, or even distance, can leave you feeling like the ground has been pulled out from under you. Grief is messy. It can feel like sadness one day, anger the next, and numbness the day after. And sometimes you may wonder if you'll ever feel whole again.

Even Jesus understood grief—He wept when His friend Lazarus died. He knows what it means to feel the sting of loss and He promises comfort for those who mourn. Grief isn't something you "get over." It's something you learn to walk through with God by your side.

God doesn't ask you to hide your pain or pretend to be strong. He invites you to bring your broken heart to Him because He is close to the brokenhearted and saves those crushed in spirit (Psalm 34:18). The hurt may never fully disappear, but His presence can help you carry it.

Heart Check

1. What loss in your life still feels heavy to carry?

____

____

____

____

____

____

2. How do you usually express your grief—by crying, writing, praying, or holding it in?

____

____

____

____

____

3. What does it mean to you that Jesus also wept?

____

____

____

____

____

____

Let's Pray

God, my heart is heavy and sometimes I don't even know what to say. The grief feels like too much to bear. But You promise to comfort me, even in my deepest pain. Help me not to shut You out but to let You in. Hold me close when I feel broken and remind me that I'm never alone in my hurt. Amen.

Girl, Write This Down

- God, here's what I've lost and why it hurts...
- When I feel this pain, this is how I want to learn to lean on You...
- One small way I can honor the person (or thing) I've lost is...

My Honest Thoughts

____

____

____

____

What I Am Praying For

____

____

____

____

What God Has Shown Me

____

____

____

____

Chapter 23

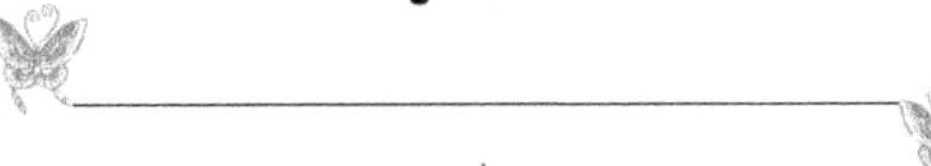

Dreaming Forward

"Commit to the Lord whatever you do, and he will establish your plans."
Proverbs 16:3 (NIV)

College, Career, and Calling

Thinking about the future can feel exciting—and overwhelming. Should you go to college, start a career, or pursue another path? While the choices may seem big, remember that God cares about your future more than you do. He has already mapped out a plan for your life.

Your role is to pray, seek wise advice, and commit your plans to Him. God's will isn't about stress—it's about trust. When you place your future in His hands, you can move forward with confidence, knowing that every step can be guided by His wisdom.

Heart Check

1. What dreams do you have for your future?

____

____

____

____

2. Who can you talk to for wise advice about college or career choices?

____

____

____

____

3. What does committing your plans to God look like?

____

____

____

____

Let's Pray

God, thank You for having a plan for my future. Help me to trust You as I make decisions about school, career, and life. Show me the right path and give me peace in the process. Amen.

Girl, Write This Down

- A dream I have for my future is...

- One step I can take toward that dream is...

- What does committing my plans to God look like?

My Honest Thoughts

____

____

____

____

What I Am Praying For

____

____

____

____

What God Has Shown Me

____

____

____

____

ADDENDUM

Real Prayers for Real Struggles

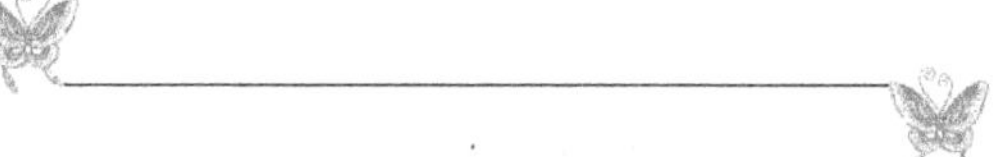

Sometimes, life hits hard and you need help right now. Here are some short, powerful prayers for real situations.

When I Feel Anxious

"Do not be anxious about anything, but in every situation, by prayer and petition, with thanksgiving, present your requests to God. And the peace of God, which transcends all understanding, will guard your hearts and your minds in Christ Jesus." – Philippians 4:6–7 (NIV)

Prayer:

God, my thoughts are racing and my heart feels heavy. Help me breathe. Calm my mind and remind me You're in control. Replace my anxiety with Your peace.

When I'm Angry

"My dear brothers and sisters, take note of this: Everyone should be quick to listen, slow to speak and slow to become angry, because human anger does not produce the righteousness that God desires." – James 1:19–20 (NIV)

Prayer:

Lord, I feel so frustrated and upset. Help me not to say or do anything I'll regret. Teach me how to cool down and handle this with grace.

When I feel Depressed

"The Lord is close to the brokenhearted and saves those who are crushed in spirit." – Psalm 34:18 (NIV)

Prayer:

God, everything feels heavy and dark. Please be near. Remind me of my worth, my purpose, and that this feeling won't last forever.

When I'm Pressured to Fit In

"Do not conform to the pattern of this world but be transformed by the renewing of your mind. Then you will be able to test and approve what God's will is—His good, pleasing and perfect will." – Romans 12:2 (NIV)

Prayer:

Jesus, it's hard to be different. Give me strength to stay true to who I am in You. I don't want to lose myself trying to be accepted.

When a Friendship Hurts

"A friend loves at all times, and a brother is born for a time of adversity." – Proverbs 17:17 (NIV)

Prayer:

Lord, I don't understand what happened. I feel hurt and confused. Help me forgive, heal, and find friends who reflect Your love.

When I Struggle with Temptation or Addiction

"No temptation has overtaken you except what is common to mankind. And God is faithful; He will not let you be tempted beyond what you can bear. But when you are tempted, He will also provide a way out so that you can endure it." – 1 Corinthians 10:13 (NIV)

Prayer:

God, I'm struggling and it feels like I'm losing. I want to stop, but I need You to help me. Give me strength and bring people who will support me.

When I'm Struggling with Sex and Boundaries

"Do you not know that your bodies are temples of the Holy Spirit, who is in you, whom you have received from God? You are not your own; you were bought at a price. Therefore, honor God with your bodies." – 1 Corinthians 6:19–20 (NIV)

Prayer:

Lord, I have questions and desires I don't always know what to do with. Sometimes I feel pressure or confused around sex and I need Your wisdom and strength. Help me understand my worth and not base it on what others expect from me. Teach me how to make choices that honor You and protect my heart. Help me set boundaries that are healthy and right. Let me know that I don't have to give myself away to feel loved. Amen.

When I'm Afraid

"I sought the Lord, and He answered me; He delivered me from all my fears." – Psalm 34:4 (NIV)

Prayer:

God, I'm scared. Please be my courage. Help me feel safe in Your arms and strong in Your promises.

When I Need Wisdom

"If any of you lacks wisdom, you should ask God, who gives generously to all without finding fault, and it will be given to you." – James 1:5 (NIV)

Prayer:

God, I don't know what to do. I feel confused and unsure. Please give me Your wisdom and help me make choices that honor You.

When I Need Guidance

"Trust in the Lord with all your heart and lean not on your own understanding; in all your ways submit to Him, and He will make your paths straight." – Proverbs 3:5–6 (NIV)

Prayer:

Lord, I need direction. I don't want to take the wrong path. Please show me the way and help me trust You, even when I don't see the full picture.

When I Need Courage

"Have I not commanded you? Be strong and courageous. Do not be afraid; do not be discouraged, for the Lord your God will be with you wherever you go." – Joshua 1:9 (NIV)

Prayer:

God, I feel nervous and unsure, but I know You are with me. Help me be brave and walk forward in faith, even when I'm scared.

When I'm Being Bullied

"The Lord is close to the brokenhearted and saves those who are crushed in spirit." – Psalm 34:1B (NIV)

Prayer:

God, when people are mean to me, talk behind my back, or try to make me feel small, it hurts deeply. Sometimes I feel like no one understands what I'm going through. But You see it all. Help me to remember that my worth comes from You, not from what they say or do. Give me courage to speak up when I need to and surround me with people who love me the way You do. Let me feel safe, seen, and strong in You. Amen.

When I've Thought About Suicide

"For I know the plans I have for you," says the Lord. "They are plans for good and not for disaster, to give you a future and a hope."– Jeremiah 29:11 (NIV)

Prayer:

God, sometimes the pain feels too heavy and I wonder if it would be easier to give up. But deep inside, I want to believe that my life matters. I want to believe You created me for a reason. Help me hold on. Help me find someone to talk to and not hide what I'm feeling. Remind me that this moment is not the end of my story. Speak life and hope into me right now. I need You, God. Please stay with me. Amen.

When I Feel Lonely

"Be strong and courageous, for the Lord your God goes with you; He will never leave you nor forsake you." – Deuteronomy 31:6 (NIV)

Prayer:

Lord, I feel so alone. Even when I'm around people, it's like I don't really belong. I need a friend who understands, who sees me for who I am. Thank You for always being near, even when others aren't. Please send people into my life who are kind, honest, and true. Teach me to be a good friend too. And help me remember that being alone doesn't mean I am unloved. I belong to You. Amen.

When I'm Struggling with My Faith in God

"I do believe; help me overcome my unbelief." – Mark 9:24 (NIV)

Prayer:

God, sometimes I wonder if You're really there. I don't always feel You and life gets so confusing. It's hard to trust when things don't make sense. But something in me still wants to believe. Please show Yourself to me in real ways. Give me peace when I doubt and patience as I grow. I am trying, Lord. Help me believe. Amen.

Here is hope for the struggle. You are not alone.

No matter what you're facing—pain, pressure, confusion, or fear—God sees you. He's not afraid of your questions, your mess, or your doubts. In fact, He welcomes them. His love is not based on how perfect you are. It's based on how perfect His love is.

If you're struggling right now, don't keep it in. Reach out to someone you trust: a parent, a mentor, a teacher, a pastor, or even a friend. Sometimes the bravest thing you can do is say, "I need help."

Remember this:

You are not forgotten

You are deeply loved

You are still becoming who God created you to be.

Keep praying, even when it feels hard. Keep reaching, even when it feels lonely. Keep believing, even when you don't have all the answers. God is writing a beautiful story with your life.

Prayer Word Bank

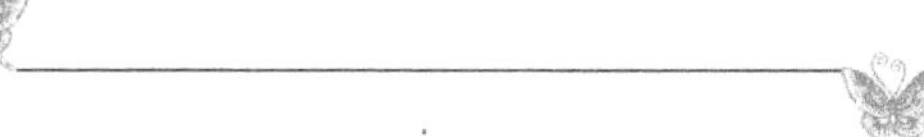

Here's a list of powerful words to help you when you're stuck. Mix and match them in your prayers!

Adoration: Holy, Mighty, Glorious, Awesome, Worthy, Sovereign

Gratitude: Thank You, Grateful, Blessed, Appreciate, Praise

Help: Strength, Peace, Courage, Protection, Guidance, Wisdom

Confession: Sorry, Forgive me, Cleanse, Renew, Honest, Real

Faith: Trust, Believe, Hope, Confident, Unshaken, Promise

Worship: Sing, Glory, Lift, Exalt, Honor, Bow

Relationship: Father, Friend, Savior, Healer, Redeemer, King

You don't have to use all the words. Just find the ones that speak to you—and speak them to God.

About the Author

Cynthia M. Pillow is a faith-filled mentor, speaker, and the founder of *Pure Beauty GEM*, a Christ-centered organization empowering girls to discover their identity, purpose, and voice through God. With a heart for teen girls and a passion for prayer, Cynthia wrote *Girl, Pray* to help young women find the courage to talk to God in honest, powerful ways—no perfection required.

She lives in Suitland, Maryland with her husband, William and has two adult children, Kevin and Celena and one grandson Ethan. Her daughter, Celena, serves as co-founder of *Pure Beauty GEM* and is part of the legacy Cynthia is building—one generation of strong, faith-filled girls at a time.

This is Cynthia's debut book but certainly not her last. She believes every girl deserves to be seen, heard, and spiritually anchored in who God says she is.

About Pure Beauty GEM

Established in 2015 (10 years), Pure Beauty GEM stands for God's Exceptionally Made Girl, a mentoring and empowerment ministry for girls aged seven to 17 founded by Cynthia M. Pillow and co-led by her daughter Celena. The organization is about building and strengthening relationships between mothers and daughters, women and girls, mentors and mentees. The organization's mandate is to equip girls with biblical truth, real-life tools, and a loving community to grow into confident, Christ-centered young women.

Through workshops, Bible studies, events, and mentorship, Pure Beauty GEM creates a safe space for girls to flourish in faith, character, and purpose.

Learn more: www.purebeautygem.com

Contact: purebeautytgif1@aol.com

Follow on Facebook @Cynthia Pillow

Instagram @puregem1568

www.ingramcontent.com/pod-product-compliance
Lightning Source LLC
Chambersburg PA
CBHW060949050726
47592CB00003B/1165